TIME FOR KIDS READERS

A New Day For South Africa

by Charles Hirsch

Harcourt

Orlando   Austin   Chicago   New York   Toronto   London   San Diego

Visit *The Learning Site!*
www.harcourtschool.com

From 1948 to 1994, South Africa was ruled under a system known as apartheid (uh•PAR•tyd). The word *apartheid* means "apartness" in the Afrikaans language spoken by some white South Africans. Apartheid kept black South Africans and other people of color apart from white South Africans.

By the 1990s South Africa had 32 million black people and six million white people. Yet black people didn't have a voice. They weren't allowed to vote. They went to separate schools, lived in separate neighborhoods, and used separate transportation. This is the story of one man who helped change the lives of all people in South Africa.

A sign points to separate camping sections for white people and people of color. Such separations were the law until 1994.

South Africa is a land of great natural beauty.

"By investing in the youth, you are investing in the future."
—*Nelson Mandela*

THE MAKING OF A LEADER

What is Africa? It is a land of countless sights and sounds. It is made up of more than 50 countries. It is an ancient land rich in culture. It is thousands of groups of people speaking thousands of different languages. It has the world's longest river—the crocodile-filled Nile. It has the world's largest desert, the Sahara. It has rain forests and 12,000-pound (5,443-kg) elephants. Africa is the home continent of one of the twentieth century's heroes: Nelson Mandela.

Nelson Rolihlahla (ROH•lee•hla•hlah) Mandela was born on July 18, 1918. He was born deep in the province of Transkei (trans•KAY) in the village of Mvezo. Mandela's family moved to Qunu (KOO•nou) when he was an infant.

Qunu is a village of clans of the large Tembu (TEM•boo) tribe. The Tembu lived in clusters of homesteads scattered across Transkei. The region takes its name from the Kei River. When Mandela was a boy, eroded land, streams, cattle tracks, and a rutted road crisscrossed Qunu. Every now and then young Mandela and the other village children would run out in excitement to see the vehicles that occasionally came through the village.

Mandela's boyhood was peaceful. He spent his days tilling fields and herding cattle. At night he listened to the tribal elders talk of the time before white people came to that part of South Africa. When Rolihlahla Mandela was a child, no one imagined that he—or any other black person—would ever be elected president of South Africa.

Mandela's father was a Thembu chief and an adviser to the Thembu tribal rulers. Rolihlahla Mandela was not in line to become a king. He was groomed, like his father before him, to become a lawyer.

In 1994, Nelson Mandela visited the village of his childhood.

By the age of six, Mandela was a herder, looking after goats, sheep, and cattle in the fields. He learned to use a slingshot and to gather wild honey, fruits, and edible roots. He would drink warm milk fresh from the cow, swim in icy streams, and catch fish with a homemade line and hook. From those days in Qunu, he says in his autobiography, *Long Walk to Freedom,* came his love of the open grassy plains, "the simple beauties of nature, the clean line of the horizon."

Mandela started school at seven years old. At primary school his teacher thought his name should sound more British, so she changed it to Nelson. Even as a youth, Mandela showed signs of leadership. In 1930, after the death of his father, 12-year-old Nelson was sent to live in the palace of the chief of the Thembu tribe. His intelligence quickly marked him as the one who would someday rule the tribe.

Transkei Province is where Nelson Mandela grew up.

In 1940, Mandela was expelled from Fort Hare College in the Eastern Cape for helping to organize a strike. Mandela had protested the college's efforts to limit the power of the student council. Then he headed for the city of Johannesburg, where he worked briefly as a guard at a gold mine. At the same time as he got a job as a clerk in a law office, he began studying for his law degree.

During the 1940s, he began to see the daily cruelties of apartheid. Under this system, black people had no rights in the eyes of the government. Deep inside, Mandela began to feel a need to change his world. He knew he could have the easy life of a lawyer in the rural setting that was his childhood home. Instead, he chose a course for his life that would lead to sacrifice and suffering for his cause.

Nelson Mandela studied hard and was one of the few black South Africans to become a lawyer.

In 1944 Mandela and two close friends, Oliver Tambo and Walter Sisulu, formed the Youth League of the African National Congress (ANC). The African National Congress was a group organized in 1912 to act against white rule.

Mandela became involved in programs of nonviolent resistance—peaceful protests. He and other members of the Youth League protested against the laws that forced black South Africans to carry passes. "It was a time when we talked about nothing but politics," recalls Amina Cachalia, who helped organize protests.

During this time, Mandela married Evelyn Ntoko Mase, a nurse, but the marriage was troubled. Evelyn Mandela wanted her husband to concentrate on his law career and forget politics. Mandela was growing angrier at the discrimination against black South Africans that he witnessed daily. Nelson and Evelyn Mandela separated in 1955 and divorced two years later.

In December 1956 police arrested Mandela and 155 other activists. The white authorities charged them with treason, or working against their country. Mandela and others had staged strikes and protests against apartheid laws. They accused Mandela and the others of betraying South Africa. After a more than four-year trial—during which time Mandela married Nomzamo Winifred "Winnie" Madikizela—he was found not guilty.

Mandela gave up nonviolent protest to form the military part of the ANC. The ANC then began a series of bombings of power plants, rail lines, and military targets. Mandela traveled to many countries to find support for the ANC. More than a year later, police captured Mandela.

A life of separation began for Nelson and Winnie. "He told me . . . that there would never be a normal situation where he would be head of the family," Winnie Mandela recalled. "He told me this in great pain. I was completely shattered."

Nelson and Winnie Mandela after their wedding.

Nelson Mandela was one of many people charged with treason in 1956. He stands here with others who also went on trial.

"The wounds that cannot be seen are more painful than those that can be treated by a doctor."

—Nelson Mandela reflecting on his visit to his former prison, Robben Island, February 1994

FROM PRISONER 466/64 TO FREEDOM

Soon after his arrest and return to South Africa in 1962, Nelson Mandela was put on trial. He was charged first for urging protests and then for plotting revolution. In 1964, while already in jail, he was convicted of treason. He was also charged with the destruction that resulted from the ANC bombings.

At his 1962 trial Mandela served as his own lawyer. His defense came down to this basic idea. "I consider myself neither legally nor morally bound to obey laws made by a Parliament [lawmaking body] in which I have no representation," Mandela argued. "There comes a time," he concluded at the end of his trial, "as it came in my life, when a man is denied the right to live a normal life, when he can only live the life of an outlaw because the government has so decreed to use the law to impose a state of outlawry upon him." Mandela's punishment was to be in prison for life.

While he was a prisoner, Nelson Mandela sewed clothes.

In His Own Words

After 28 years in prison, Nelson Mandela was finally released. Many of those years were harsh and cruel. Often there seemed to be no hope of returning to the outside world, of being free. Here he recalls the day he was freed from prison, February 11, 1990.

"I woke up at the usual time, between half past four and five o'clock. I carried on with my normal routine. I had ample time to do exercises. I ran around, did some press-ups, some abdominal exercises, rope skipping, and got on the bicycle. Then I had breakfast. I ate alone. Normally I just take some cereal and some skimmed milk. And I had a routine medical checkup from the prison doctor.

"Leading comrades came to see me early in the morning. They returned with my wife and members of my family for the purpose of escorting me. We were supposed to leave the prison at three o'clock. But we actually left at four. When we approached the gate, we got out and I was alarmed to find such a large crowd. I couldn't even greet my friends. I couldn't find them. Then we left the prison.

"We took a roundabout route to Cape Town, which I enjoyed a great deal. I saw crowds of whites who raised the fist [to show support]. That took me by surprise. I didn't expect whites in that area to be so involved in our antiapartheid struggle. There was one family that showed tremendous excitement as we approached. I asked to stop. We shook hands, and I thanked them for coming to give me support.

"We had a very harrowing experience. Just before we reached City Hall, they asked us to drive around so we wouldn't actually be seen by the crowd. Winnie and I were sitting in the back. Suddenly, we found ourselves surrounded. They were pressing the car from all sides. We were very anxious. It was hot and oppressive. I was very concerned, of course, about Winnie. The car was rocking. The crowds were pressing. It took more than 30 minutes before we managed to reverse.

"Eventually, we got to City Hall. It was after seven when I actually went to the podium. Much to my surprise, I had forgotten my glasses in prison, so I used my wife's. They worked. I was very overwhelmed by the amount of support and enthusiasm.

"I thought about going down to [the place] where I was born and brought up. . . . I was keen to see things, to go to see the rocks on which I had played, to see whether they were as big as they were when I was a child. After school you rounded up sheep and cattle. To relive that type of life was one of my desires in prison. And of course this desire burned more fiercely the first day I came out."

—From an interview with Scott MacLeod, *LIFE* Magazine

For 18 years Nelson Mandela was simply prisoner 466/64 at Robben Island. This maximum-security prison is a craggy, wind-swept island near Cape Town harbor. Most days Mandela and other inmates were put to work with sledgehammers to break rocks into gravel for the roads around the prison. Later they were sent to work in the island's limestone quarry. The broiling African sun created a painful glare in the limestone quarry. It permanently damaged Mandela's vision.

Mandela's first prison cell was a seven-by-seven-foot cubicle. It had one dim lightbulb hanging overhead. The bed was a mat on the ground. The diet was mainly corn porridge and a bad tasting drink made of ground corn that was baked and then brewed.

Mandela never placed decorations on the walls of his cell; that way it would never feel like home. At mail call he resisted rushing forward. He would not let his jailers know how much he missed his family. Mandela tried to make the best of the 18 years he spent on the island. He wasn't allowed to read newspapers until 1980. He and the other ANC members managed to keep track of developments in South Africa through smuggled messages. In the evening they talked politics, instructing new prisoners in their political beliefs. The ANC members were such effective teachers that the prison became known as Mandela University.

Today Mandela's prison cell on Robben Island is a tourist attraction.

Mandela was not forgotten while in prison. Supporters in England were among many who asked for Mandela's release.

Mandela also found comfort in the island's stark natural beauty, in breathing the fresh air, and in observing birds and sea life. The rock formations in the quarry where he worked inspired him to study books on geology. He exercised regularly, and eventually he was allowed to play tennis. He and other prisoners held their own version of the Olympic Games.

But life in prison took its toll. Winnie was allowed only a half-hour visit with him every six months. "Had it not been for your visits, wonderful letters, and love, I would have fallen apart many years ago," he wrote her in a 1979 letter.

In 1982 authorities moved Mandela to Pollsmoor Maximum Security Prison in Cape Town. This was done to prevent him from talking about the antiapartheid movement to the other inmates at Robben Island. Mandela spent much of the next six years without being allowed to speak to his political friends.

In 1988 he was hospitalized with a severe case of tuberculosis, a serious lung disease. After he recovered, he was taken to the Victor Verster Prison Farm near Cape Town. He spent the next two years there. Prison life was easier at the prison farm. He was given his own cottage. Still, he once again took up the energetic routine that he had followed during much of his prison life. Each morning at Victor Verster, he would wake up at 3:30 A.M. and exercise for two hours—lifting weights, doing push-ups, riding a stationary bicycle, skipping rope, and jogging in place. He would then read through the morning papers and watch a TV news program, *Good Morning South Africa*.

During a 1994 visit to his former prison cell, Nelson Mandela points out things he had seen from his prison window.

Mandela visits the quarry at Robben Island where he had been once forced to work as a prisoner.

15

As Mandela's prison conditions changed, the political situation in South Africa was changing as well. Inside and outside the prison walls, the voices against apartheid would not be silenced. The younger generation was taking on the antiapartheid cause. The black majority in South Africa was becoming increasingly powerful. Throughout the free world, protests against apartheid were also growing.

In 1986 South African President P. W. Botha asked Mandela to participate in secret talks with the government. At the same time, the South African government began showing its desire to hold talks about South Africa's future. In 1989 the next president of South Africa, F. W. de Klerk, increased discussions between members of his cabinet and Mandela. President de Klerk started allowing Mandela to have visits with antiapartheid activists.

People of many political beliefs attended ANC rallies once the group was declared legal.

On February 11, 1990, de Klerk finally set Mandela free. De Klerk also lifted the ban on the ANC. When Nelson Mandela walked out of Victor Verster Prison, he looked gray and thin. Still, the sight of him set off a wave of rejoicing across South Africa. "I was completely overwhelmed by the enthusiasm," Mandela said. "It is something I did not expect."

Nelson Mandela had endured the harshness of prison life with dignity. Now he had to fill the weighty role of a leader with an equal measure of skill. He felt he must help bring democracy and equality to a deeply divided country. It was a task for which he had been preparing for the past 28 years, even though he did not know whether he would ever have the chance to attempt it. Now, at last, the moment had come.

Nelson Mandela is cheered on by children after his release from prison in February 1990.

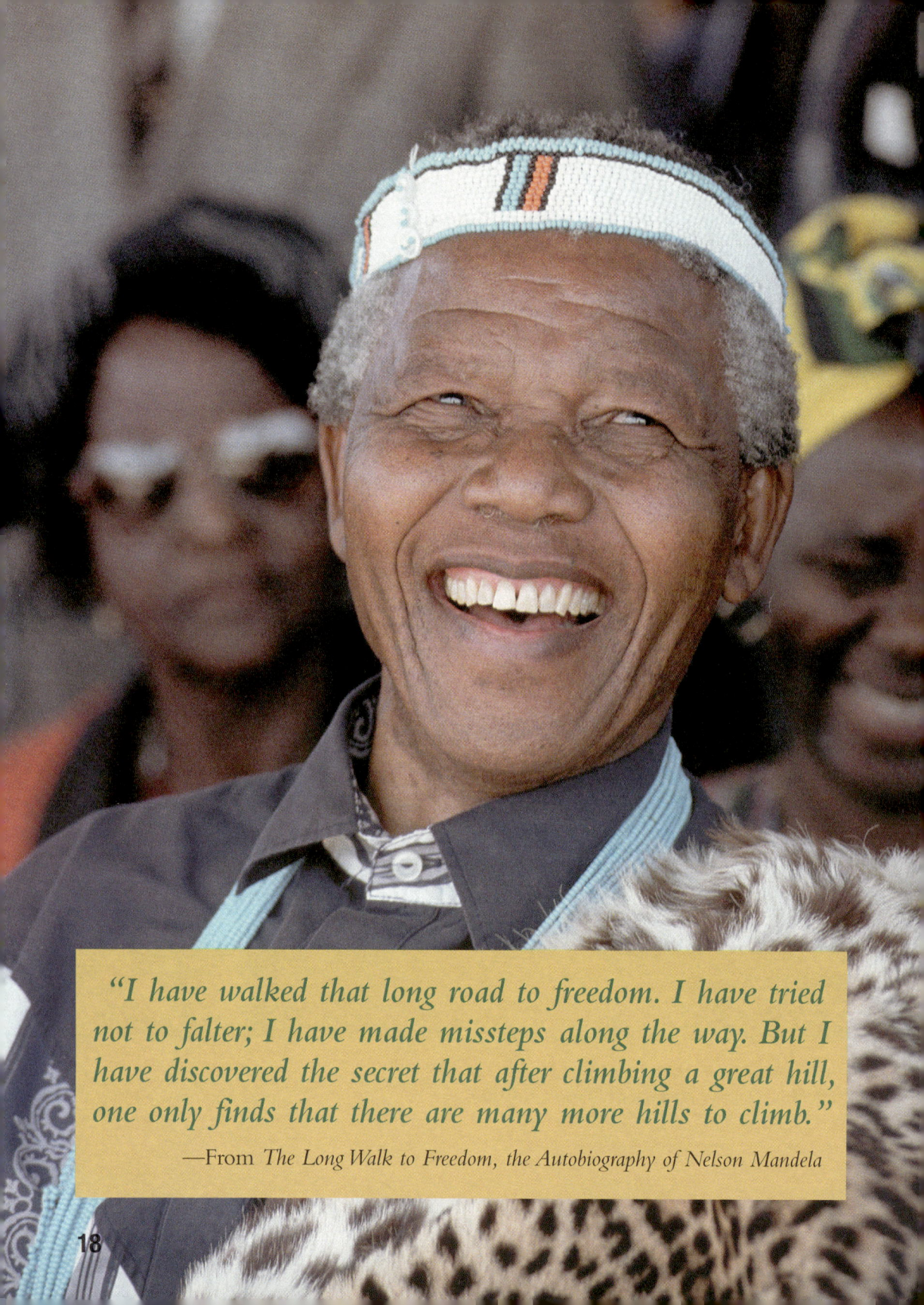

"I have walked that long road to freedom. I have tried not to falter; I have made missteps along the way. But I have discovered the secret that after climbing a great hill, one only finds that there are many more hills to climb."

—From *The Long Walk to Freedom, the Autobiography of Nelson Mandela*

A NEW DAY FOR SOUTH AFRICA

In the decade to come, the dreams of thousands of South Africans, past and present, would become reality. The chimes of freedom were ringing in eastern Europe and the Soviet Union. And, at last, the world saw Nelson Mandela come home. In the next decade the chains of apartheid, like the chains of a prisoner, would be broken. A black man would become president of South Africa.

After Nelson Mandela was set free, the real test for him and all of South Africa began. He hoped to see his country's first democratic elections. Every inch of the way, Mandela had to win the support of his own followers. More difficult still was the process of easing the fears of the government. But Mandela brought patience and wisdom to this struggle. Above all he had a sense of moral truth with which he set out to unite a divided people.

TFK DID YOU KNOW

Apartheid Means "Apartness"

Europeans first settled in what is now South Africa in 1652. They started a colony that by the end of the 1700s had about 15,000 people. These colonists set up a government and lived apart from native Africans. The colonists spoke a Dutch dialect that became known as Afrikaans. South Africa became a self-ruling country in 1910. White people remained in control.

From 1948 to 1994, the nation was ruled under a system known as apartheid. Black South Africans and others who tried to fight this system were silenced quickly and sometimes violently. Thousands were thrown in prison.

Apartheid could not last forever, though. After a long struggle, South Africa held its first open election in 1994. Once black citizens had a voice, they used it. They elected Nelson Mandela—the country's first black president.

A few months after his release, Nelson Mandela sought support from world leaders. He began a world tour. He stopped in major cities throughout the United States and Canada. In the United States he met with President George Bush. He also addressed the United States Senate and the House of Representatives. In Great Britain he met with Prime Minister Margaret Thatcher.

When he returned to South Africa, Mandela set about the work of changing South Africa into a truly democratic nation. That work began in December 1991, when he and President de Klerk established the Convention for a Democratic South Africa. The work was difficult.

Nelson Mandela met with U.S. President George Bush in 1990.

The year 1992 became a turning point. At home Mandela suffered personal hardship. While he was in prison, his wife Winnie had been his greatest supporter. At the same time, she herself had become powerful. She and her followers were later charged with criminal behavior. Mandela and his wife grew apart, and they separated in April 1992. Nelson Mandela poured himself into his nation's work. On September 26, 1992, Nelson Mandela and F.W. de Klerk signed the Record of Understanding. They formally agreed that an elected assembly would govern the new South Africa. A new constitution would be written.

At the beginning of June 1993, the country took what seemed to be a giant step toward freedom for all its citizens. More than two years after talks began, black and white political leaders announced that a free election would be held on April 27, 1994. For the first time ever, every citizen of South Africa would be able to vote. For their efforts Mandela and de Klerk were awarded the Nobel Peace Prize in 1993. The Nobel Prize is an annual international prize of great importance.

South Africa's leader, F. W. de Klerk, and Nelson Mandela announce an agreement for a "new" South Africa.

Nelson Mandela became a candidate for president. He ran against F. W. de Klerk. Few seemed surprised when Mandela won. In his autobiography he recalled the day of his election. "Great lines of patient people snaking through the dirt roads and streets of towns and cities; old women who had waited half a century to cast their first vote saying that they felt like human beings for the first time in their lives; white men and women saying they were proud to live in a free country at last."

For South Africa's black people, the elections brought an end to the injustice and injury of the past four decades. At the same time it was the beginning of a new day for South Africa. For many that new day is still dawning.

As president, Mandela's greatest accomplishment was his ability to bring about tolerance and understanding. He included representatives from all parties and races in his cabinet. Some people, however, disagreed with Mandela's actions. He set out to rewrite every apartheid regulation and put the new laws into effect.

Lines of people wait to vote in the South African election in 1994.

Nelson Mandela retired in 1999 and returned to Qunu. His retirement home is not the thatched hut of his boyhood days. Rutted roads no longer crisscross Qunu. Mandela's home is a modern, two-story mansion. It stands on high ground along the national highway. In the rolling fields at the rear of the property are his cattle, gifts from grateful followers. Mandela lives there with his wife, Graca, whom he met after his divorce from Winnie.

Though he was not born to be a king, Nelson Mandela needs no crown to be honored in the country where his long walk to freedom began. He suffered insults and injury with dignity. He governed with humility. In the process, he set an example of hope for people of all nations. He struggled all his adult life to create a new day in South Africa. Now, all these years later, the work has really just begun. "We have not taken the final step of our journey, but the first step on a longer and even more difficult road.... The true test of our devotion to freedom is just beginning," said Nelson Mandela.

TFK DID YOU KNOW

Nelson Mandela's Life Milestones

July 18, 1918	Born in Qunu, South Africa
1944	Joins the antiapartheid African National Congress (ANC)
1956–61	Put on trial for actions against the government, but declared not guilty
1962–90	Imprisoned for high treason and sabotage
1990	Released from prison
1991	Becomes President of the ANC
1993	Shares the Nobel Peace Prize with South African President F.W. de Klerk for efforts to end apartheid
1994	Elected South Africa's President
1999	Retires from the presidency